#SPORTS tweet

What I Learned from Coaches About Sports and Life

By Ronnie Lott with Keith Potter
Foreword by Sean Payton

First Printing: August 2010
Paperback ISBN: 978-1-61699-032-9 (1-61699-032-5)
eBook ISBN: 978-1-61699-033-6 (1-61699-033-3)
Place of Publication: Silicon Valley, California, USA
Paperback Library of Congress Number: 2010934248

Trademarks

All terms mentioned in this book that are known to be trademarks or service marks have been appropriately capitalized. Neither Happy About®, nor any of its imprints, can attest to the accuracy of this information. Use of a term in this book should not be regarded as affecting the validity of any trademark or service mark.

Warning and Disclaimer

Every effort has been made to make this book as complete and as accurate as possible. The information provided is on an "as is" basis. The author(s), publisher, and their agents assume no responsibility for errors or omissions. Nor do they assume liability or responsibility to any person or entity with respect to any loss or damages arising from the use of information contained herein.

Advance Praise

"This book is a fun read and Ronnie touches on great points!"
Marcus Allen, Heisman Trophy Winner and NFL Hall of Fame Member

---

"Ronnie is a winner in life. You will learn, as I have, about what it means to be a role model, proud parent, and the hardest working person to better your team. Winning is his life and he embodies greatness."
Baron Davis, Star NBA Point Guard

"Growing up watching football, I was always drawn to Ronnie Lott. The way he played, the way he leads, and the way he carries himself has always been an inspiration to me and many of my friends and teammates. Doesn't matter if you're an athlete, a fan, or somewhere in between, bottom line is you can learn from and be inspired by Ronnie Lott's insightful life lessons."
Ray Lewis, Eleven-Time NFL Pro Bowl Selection and Super Bowl Most Valuable Player

---

"I think Ronnie's the greatest of all time. He's helped me immensely by teaching me the nuances of the safety position as I start my NFL career. Ronnie's work ethic and attention to detail were the building blocks for him mastering his craft, and I think this book will help people see into the life of somebody who epitomizes greatness both on and off the field."
Taylor Mays, Safety, San Francisco 49ers

"I thoroughly enjoyed reading Ronnie's book on champions. My son is a high school football coach and I insisted that he and his players need to read it. It's a great building block to help young adults understand the sacrifices it takes to be a champion on the field and in life."
Sandy Sandoval, Senior Director, EA Sports Marketing

"This book of sports tweets is very inspirational, great reading, and very credible coming from a proven Hall of Famer like Ronnie Lott."
Daniel M. Snyder, Owner, Washington Redskins

"Ronnie Lott was one of those classic players who would have excelled in any era, and this book offers insight that is just as timeless."
Ken Whisenhunt, Head Coach, Arizona Cardinals

Dedication

This book is dedicated to my wife, Karen, and to my kids—Ryan, Hailey, Isaiah, and Chloe—for their love and support. They teach me how to make great plays every day!

Acknowledgments

I would first like to thank all of my coaches for teaching me to play the game the right way, and to my teammates who pushed me to be the best I could be.

I would like to thank Coach Robinson for teaching me to exhaust my competitive spirit.

And to my friend Marcus Allen—I never would have been able to see greatness without having been around such greatness.

Thank you to the DeBartolos. You are simply the best.

To the Walsh family—your dad pushed us to excellence!

To my friend Joe—nobody handled adversity better than you! Thank you for your friendship and for teaching me how to be patient under pressure.

Thank you to Eric Scoggins who taught me that you have to stand for something or you will fall for anything.

Thank you to Jeff Bayer who took the Hall of Fame photo.

Why Did We Write This Book?

Like all of you, I'm exploring the new media. Communication is important. It conveys our values, perspectives, and passions. If there's a new path to communicating, then I want to find it and use it.

This tweet format highlights the "aha" moments of life. It allows us to trim away needless words and give nuggets of truth and inspiration that will help us improve and search out our destiny.

As for sports, I've been a fan for life. My dad coached me from the earliest days, "get back up and try again" when I fell down. As my Little League coach, he told me that it's okay to strike out, "as long as you learn from it." It's words like those, from people like my dad, that make this book a reminder that sports really do prepare us for the bigger arenas of life.

As you read, you'll see how many of the coaches in my life challenged and inspired me to live into my potential. Imagine playing for Bill Walsh and John Robinson. But there were other coaches too, from childhood all the way through my career, and each taught me something. I've been trying to pay attention and put their lessons into practice.

This book will bring out the best in you if you give each simple tweet a chance to sink in. I'm eager to hear how it helps you and to learn from your "tweets"—the lessons you're gaining about your sport, your passion, and your life.

Let's make this pact: for the rest of our lives, we'll choose words and ways that make this world better. Read on, and may this journey take you to places where dreams and opportunities come true.

Ronnie Lott and Keith Potter

What I Learned from Coaches About Sports and Life

Contents

Foreword by Sean Payton

"Winning takes talent; to repeat takes character." Those are the words of the late, legendary coach John Wooden. Few can argue that Coach Wooden knew how to win consistently. After all, he won ten NCAA Men's Basketball National Championships in a twelve-year span. Seven of those championships came back-to-back. Coach Wooden's legend is a case study in sustaining excellence.

Sustaining excellence is the challenge for everyone who competes. Our 2009 New Orleans Saints won Super Bowl XLIV. It was a journey that started almost four years earlier, after the most devastating natural disaster in United States history hit the city of New Orleans. The story of the revival of a city and a team has been told numerous times. The journey was wrought with adversity—annual evacuations, relocating family members on a moment's notice, making tough decisions, facing uncharted waters. Those were our off-the-field challenges.

On the field, we built a talented team. After all, you do need talent to win a Super Bowl. But the word that stands out most in John Wooden's comment is character.

Character is the underlying force in our team's success. Character has guided us through those uncharted waters off the field. Character guided us through losing streaks on the field and toward a championship season.

By design, when our team references character, integrity, and discipline, we look to former players and coaches as guides. Ronnie Lott embodies all of those traits. When he told our team in early 2009 that he "smelled greatness," our players listened and believed.

When the final story is written about our New Orleans Saints, the success we can be most proud of will be the character of our players, coaches, and organization. Winning takes talent. That will never be questioned. Winning consistently, however, is built on the character of your team.

Sean Payton
Head Coach
New Orleans Saints

Section 1

Learning from a Legend

More than a legend, Bill Walsh was an extraordinary person and a genius who brought innovation and excellence to the game.

1

Don't be intimidated by teams that are bigger, stronger, or tougher. There's more to winning than size and strength.

2

Be quicker than
your opponent, and
hit them before they're
ready to be hit.

3

Pursue excellence...no, pursue perfection. You might not get to perfection, but the pursuit will take you to the top.

4

Winning is an attitude. It even matters how you put on your uniform.

5

Win with class. And, even though it's normal to hate losing, lose with class.

6

Racial diversity always means something. Think about your teammates; really appreciate each other, and even your differences.

7

Learn to execute a
game plan and you can
run any organization.

8

The purpose of the first twenty plays is to relax, to know what to expect, and to learn what needs to be done to finish well.

9

Get me two stops and two first downs in the fourth quarter; that should be enough to win. The fourth quarter is where life gets decided.

10

Ball security matters, so offense also plays defense. Field position matters, so defense also plays offense. We are all one team.

11

On the road, you must control the crowd. That means being ahead in the fourth quarter, and it means poise when the stadium gets loud.

12

A road trip is a business trip. That's all. Don't get distracted. Do your job.

13

The West Coast offense is like a basketball fast break; there's a style and a pace to it. It moves with a very clear purpose!

14

A sense of humor cuts tension and shakes out fear. The best teams laugh when they can.

Section II

From a Team of Coaches

Other 49er coaches, like Ray Rhodes and George Siefert, made a huge difference in my game and in my life.

15

Famous coaches, like famous players, aren't the whole picture. There's always someone else bringing something to the table.

16

The coach's job is to teach the game and then to let the players play the game.

17

The head coach is the architect and the mobilizer. The assistants have to be hands-on and right in the mix with the players.

18

If you're the head coach, build a strong team of assistants. Eventually they'll launch and take their own teams, and they'll be part of your legacy.

19

You want assistants who own your basic values; but dare to hire people who are strong where you are weak.

20

Get the right mix of coaches
and leaders on the field
playing the roles that fit
them perfectly—greatness.

21

Fly around on defense.
"Play with passion."

22

Don't have tight rear ends. You're
gonna get beat sometimes, but don't
play like you're afraid of getting beat.

23

The great secondary strips
the ball, and every team
needs playmakers!

24

Never come to work without bringing your lunch pail. There's no free lunch.

25

Rookies have to buy—and do some grunt work. No fun for the rookies, but it helps keep things in perspective.

26

Discipline is what it takes to be an All-Pro.

27

Backpedal and read the quarterback at the same time. It sounds like nothing, but simple fundamentals make all the difference.

What I Learned from Coaches About Sports and Life

Section III

Running with Champions

When we're surrounded by peers who are committed to greatness, they become our coaches too.

28

Great players raise the bar. They demand the best out of me simply by being phenomenal.

29

Joe Montana proved that even one second is enough time for a miracle; you still have a shot to win. Don't stop believing!

30

Passion helps. But when everyone is fired up, I want the guy who can stay cool on my side.

31

Learn from people who are better than you, and even from those who aren't.

32

When you stop learning,
you start dying.

33

Joe Montana said, "Get me the ball
two more times and we'll win." We
believed him because he believed in
himself. That's leadership.

34

Joe Montana used to throw rolls of tape into the holes in the top of the goalpost. To Joe, being accurate meant everything.

35

In training camp, I learned to watch my bicycle—or else it would end up in a tree! Success isn't all business. Friendship and laughter help.

36

If anyone can prove that it pays to work hard every day, it's Jerry Rice. Greatness never rests.

37

They used to say the singer James Brown was "the hardest working man in show business." Jerry Rice was the James Brown of football.

38

Sometimes, greatness is about accountability. We love each other too much to allow compromise.

39

Every time Jerry Rice saw a white line, he got both feet down. If you don't stay in bounds, it doesn't count—anywhere.

40

Jerry Rice honestly believed that if his hands could get close to the ball, then the ball should be caught. No excuses.

41

Talk about Joe's poise, Jerry's brilliance, Dwight's catch, or Roger's toughness. But in our hearts, we know that the other guys got us there.

Section IV

Lessons from the Hall

The Hall of Fame is a great honor, an amazing fraternity, and a school for lessons on greatness.

42

Around Hall of Famers, you feel the intensity, since every guy in the Hall wants to be the best.

43

It hurts to know we can't do everything athletically that we used to do; but we can still be great at something.

44

Jim Brown taught me how glad I am that I wasn't born in his era—too tough to bring down. Old-school toughness is a good thing.

45

The one guy who hit me harder than I hit him? Walter Payton. Some called him "Sweetness," but that's not the word that I use.

46

Seeing Earl Campbell come charging into the backfield was a serious test of my manhood. I'd say I passed the test, but I can't remember.

47

It's possible to be the toughest guy on the field and the nicest guy off the field. If you need evidence, look at Merlin Olsen.

48

Steve Largent taught me
humility. No one could
stop him. He just knew how
to get open. Add innate
ability to precise patterns,
and look out.

49

Dick Butkus taught me to BE Dick Butkus. It's like a kid playing dress-up; you pretend that you are someone until you grow into it....

50

If I could have played football with Ray Nitschke even one time, I'd be better for it. Some people make you better by association.

51

James Lofton and
Ahmad Rashad took me
under their wings at my
rookie Pro Bowl. They made
sure I knew how to be a man.
We all need mentors.

52

Art Shell is the epitome of the quiet warrior. He reminds me of the scripture, "In quietness and confidence is my strength."

53

Never forget that once you get in the Hall of Fame—whatever the sport or enterprise—there are things you have to do to stay there.

54

Whatever your last day of football, we all have something in common: there comes that moment and it hurts.

Section V

Trojan Pride

Before Bill Walsh, I had John Robinson, along with Norv Turner, Dennis Thurmond, Don Lindsey, and Bob Toledo.

55

USC gave me an amazing heritage—great coaches and rich tradition. Being a Trojan taught me life lessons that I will carry forever.

56

John Robinson taught us
how to get respect every
time we lined up—compete
in everything you do.

57

Even if we lost, Coach Robinson got through to me that I can still win the battle with the guy across from me. Not a win, but something.

58

According to Coach Robinson, Lynn Swann could climb to the top of a goalpost to catch a football. Legends have an ounce of truth.

59

When we lost, Coach Robinson always said that it was his fault, not ours. "I didn't do enough to get you ready." That's leadership.

60

At USC, I learned to love
defense. You can't always
control how offense is
clicking. On defense, you just
dig deeper and hit harder.

61

Ray Gous taught me to be a USC Trojan for life: "We don't die; we just multiply!"

62

Being around USC taught me—parents, listen up—that if you can get near the periphery of greatness, some of it is bound to rub off.

Section VI

Friday Night Lights and Other Childhood Lessons

Coach Christopher at Eisenhower High School, along with my dad, fed me the passion and laid out the game plan.

63

Who can forget two-a-days
in the late summer?
I remember the guys who
quit—but just barely.

64

I can still smell the bus exhaust from chugging to the Orange Show in San Bernardino. It comes back like yesterday, being part of a team.

65

A kid has to dream. Even if dreams don't all come true, we're all better off for dreaming.

66

I remember lying on the high school gym floor, feeling butterflies and letting the coach stoke us. I still look for moments like that.

67

"Keep your eye on the ball." Dad said it first. Others said the same in a thousand ways. Keep your focus. Stay on track. Live with purpose.

68

Get ready to work. The best things in life don't come easy.

69

Get out of bed. Champions are made in the morning, while other people are sleeping.

70

"Listen to your coaches and treat them with respect, or else you answer to me." That's what a kid needs to hear from his dad.

71

Dad taught me to keep showing up and to keep working. He taught me by doing it. Every kid needs to see this in action.

72

My dad is a big supporter, but he's not overly impressed. I think he'd be proud if I were a really reliable plumber.

73

Dad showed me how to exhaust life; how to put it all out there, so at the end of the game—or life—you have no regrets.

74

"Take care of your brother and sister." I can hear Dad saying it. "And provide for your family." With him, those are non-negotiables.

75

I'm still learning, but Dad tried to teach me to like everything. It reminds me of the janitor who considers every day an adventure.

76

From the time I first put the uniform on, I never cheated myself. In my mind, the stadium was always packed and the game was a big one.

77

Friday night lights aren't different than Sunday morning. People are a bit faster, and a bit stronger, but we all go to battle with friends.

Section VII

From My Wife and Kids

Family is like sports, forcing you
to communicate, to work through
differences, to get on the same page,
and to be a team.

78

It's not fair to live vicariously through my children's successes or failures. I'm learning to let them find their way while I support them.

79

Sports are fun, and they should be fun. Sometimes, I just like watching my kids play the game, because that's what they're doing—playing.

80

Kids' sports are the best bridge-builders. People have to learn to get along and make their differences work for them and not against them.

81

The best part of kids' sports is learning to share. Involvement in team sports is one of the surest predictors of success with people.

82

One of my sons has become a primary spiritual leader in my life. Allowing that flip-flop in roles has helped me to grow as a man.

83

Watch what happens when kids forget the fundamentals. The same thing happens to all of us.

84

My kids aren't impressed by my trophies. They don't care if I'm famous or rich. They care if I'm going to show up for them and their mom.

85

Words are powerful, especially when they come from a dad. So I want to use words well.

86

In marriage, the game is empathetic listening. That doesn't come naturally to most guys, so we have to train like mad. But it pays off.

87

It's embarrassing to admit,
but we like cheerleaders.
It means so much to
have a beautiful woman
in your corner when you
go into battle.

88

Building a family is like building a team; at the end of the day, you want everyone playing to their potential and feeling they belong.

89

As you would do with your teammates, do with your family—not everything from the locker room, but the rest of it.

90

Never underestimate what your kids can teach you and how they can empower you to find ways to be better at all that you do.

91

Continue to learn how to love. This will be our true greatness and it's what matters most in life.

Section VIII

From Other Sports

You might not believe this, but football isn't even my favorite sport—and every sport teaches.

92

Basketball is my favorite sport.
My favorite part of basketball
is getting the ball around.
Let everyone play the game.

93

My favorite players in basketball
have always been Cousy, Oscar, Tiny,
Magic, Stockton—all the guys who
know how to make others look good.

94

In basketball, I learned that you better be in great shape if you want to play with the big boys.

95

I shot an air ball in a USC basketball game. Most people don't even know I played basketball at USC. Maybe that air ball explains why!

96

"Be quick, but don't hurry." John Wooden might have said it first, but my coaches told me, too. You better move fast, but play smart.

97

What did I learn in basketball? It hurts more to shoot an air ball than to whiff on a tackle. And I should stick to football!

98

Golf is a sport that doesn't reward anger. Since football does reward anger, and life doesn't, golf has become an important teacher to me.

99

Golf is all about responding, not reacting. When we react badly to mistakes, we compound our errors. When we respond well, we play well.

100

Golf takes me back to my childhood. Growing up in D.C., we took walks around Potomac Park and the monuments. Golf is a walk in the park.

101

Golf is all about putting in the repetitions—the practice green, the range, the bunker. How do I think I'll get better without reps?

102

Playing shortstop, I was taught to get my glove all the way to the dirt and then adjust up.

103

Baseball is a game of repetition. The more groundballs you take in practice, the more likely that you'll get your glove on it in the game.

104

My baseball coach used to say, "Get to the spot, and then play the ball." Still true. You have to get there if you want to have a chance.

105

Hockey reminds me that sometimes you have to take off the gloves and fight. Not always, of course. But there are some things you have to do.

106

When I think of track and field, I think of Tommy Smith and John Carlos at the 1968 Olympics; champions in the moment of truth.

107

I haven't wrestled since junior high P.E., but I respect those who do. And I'd never want to get in the ring with Dan Gable.

108

As a kid, I'd spy on the home of Muhammad Ali, the finest athlete of all time. I wanted to get as close as I could to greatness.

Section IX

From the Coach Called Adversity

It would be nice to say I had a ring
for every finger, but losing is also
part of life—and a great teacher.

109

Adversity can make cowards, but it can also produce heroes.

110

If you don't stare adversity down, it'll take you down.

111

You have to have a short memory when it comes to adversity. When you miss a tackle, the pace of play doesn't allow you to dwell on it.

112

Joe Montana drank adversity the way most of us drink milk. The great ones live for the challenge.

113

It's okay to be wrong. Now, don't let your pride get in the way of correction.

114

Inches matter. In every game that counts, inches matter.

115

Our team was in total chaos before the Denver Super Bowl. Somehow, we still managed to win big. Keep playing through the troubles.

116

Adversity can make fear spread like a cancer in the locker room. Be part of the cure.

117

No matter how much you suffer, the world moves on. Get up and go.

118

When we won the Super Bowl my rookie year, the Steelers (winners of four Super Bowls) were so gracious in losing. Win or lose, have class!

Section X

From the Coach Called Success

If we're paying attention, success can teach us; but if we're not, it can spoil us.

119

Smelling greatness

is the essence of why

we run the race.

120

Success is not just about

you. It's bigger than that.

It can move a city and

make a whole community

feel like champions.

121

Jerry Rice used to say, "I never had the perfect game." That should say something about success. Don't stop working.

122

Reinvent success each and every time. It's never the same.

123

Always exhaust success
when you have it because
you might not see it again.

124

When you have a collective group
of people who believe in a common
goal, you can achieve anything.

125

Nobody owns success.
But you can enjoy it.

126

The bottom half of the roster truly
matters more than the star players.

127

With every successful head coach,
there comes a staff that's
even more valuable.

128

Forget about success quickly.
Improve on it. There are
always other levels.

129

We all have in common
the ability to be ordinary
or extraordinary. If you are
extraordinary, don't lose
appreciation for the ordinary.

130

Look at everybody as if they're wearing the yellow jacket—frontrunners. Never look down on people or underestimate them.

Section XI

Sports Imitates Life

The things I've learned in sports are useful for my family, my vocation, my nonprofit efforts, my friendships, and my faith.

131

I know that people can succeed without being athletes. But if you can play sports, why not? Sports are a great training ground for life.

132

I can hear my Little League coach saying, "Don't step in the bucket." Even in life, plant your back foot and step into it, whatever it is.

133

In golf, I'm in the trees a lot. I've learned to get it back in play, instead of trying to make the heroic shot through the impossible gap.

134

In sports, you want to exhaust yourself. Win or lose, you know you put it all out there. In the same way, try to exhaust life. No regrets.

135

In every sport it comes down to two things—who brings the effort and who makes the most mistakes. The same is true for other endeavors.

136

In football, you don't pace yourself. Go all out for a few seconds, catch your breath, make plans; then do it again. Try to live life this way.

137

Every field has champions: presidents, Michael Jordan, Miss America. They all share courage, resilience, and joy in what they do.

138

Life hurts and no one likes to lose. The real champions are the ones who know what to do with their disappointments.

139

Football is a string of defining moments. Who wants it more? Who paid the price? Who feels good at the end of the day?

140

Coaches can teach footwork and technique. But to really put the hit on someone, it comes from a deeper place. It's an explosion from within.

About the Authors

Roger Craig, Coach Bill Walsh, and Ronnie Lott

The name Ronnie Lott screams toughness and excellence. As a ten-time Pro Bowl selection and a first-ballot Hall of Famer, Ronnie is one of the most respected figures in professional sports. Add his four Super Bowl rings with the San Francisco 49ers to what was arguably his best season, leading the NFL in interceptions with the Oakland Raiders, and you've heard only part of the story. Off the field, Lott is known as a tireless advocate for children. His nonprofit, All Stars Helping Kids, has raised millions of dollars to improve the lives of at-risk young people. Even more, Ronnie is a coach and catalyst for other athletes who have a heart for making their communities a better place.

Keith Potter is an author, faith coach, and inspirational speaker committed to empowering champions, rejuvenating marriages, and revitalizing organizations. After leading and launching nonprofit enterprises for twenty-five years, Potter understands the passions, principles, and priorities that mobilize people for both goodness and greatness. As the creative force behind the nonprofit The Champion Project (http://www.championproject.com), Keith Potter coaches leadership teams and emerging leaders internationally. He is the consummate teacher, catalyst, and friend to influencers in numerous fields.

Other Books in the THINKaha Series

The THINKaha book series is for thinking adults who lack the time or desire to read long books, but want to improve themselves with knowledge of the most up-to-date subjects. THINKaha is a leader in timely, cutting edge books and mobile applications from relevant experts that provide valuable information in a fun, Twitter-brief format for a fast-paced world.

They are available online at http://thinkaha.com or at other online and physical bookstores.

1. *#BOOK TITLE tweet Book01*: 140 Bite-Sized Ideas for Compelling Article, Book, and Event Titles by Roger C. Parker

2. *#COACHING tweet Book01*: 140 Bite-Sized Insights On Making A Difference Through Executive Coaching by Sterling Lanier

3. *#CONTENT MARKETING tweet Book01*: 140 Bite-sized Ideas to Create and Market Compelling Content by Ambal Balakrishnan

4. *#DEATHtweet Book01*: A Well Lived Life through 140 Perspectives on Death and its Teachings by Timothy Tosta

5. *#DIVERSITYtweet Book01*: Embracing the Growing Diversity in Our World by Deepika Bajaj

6. *#DREAMtweet Book01*: Inspirational Nuggets of Wisdom from a Rock and Roll Guru to Help You Live Your Dreams by Joe Heuer

7. *#ENTRYLEVELtweet Book01*: Taking Your Career from Classroom to Cubicle by Heather R. Huhman

8. *#JOBSEARCHtweet Book01*: 140 job search nuggets for managing your career and landing your dream job by Barbara Safani

9. *#LEADERSHIPtweet Book01*: 140 bite-sized ideas to help you become the leader you were born to be by Kevin Eikenberry

10. *#LEAN STARTUP tweet Book01*: 140 Insights for Building a Lean Startup! By Seymour Duncker

11. *#MILLENNIALtweet Book01*: 140 Bite-sized Ideas for Managing the Millennials by Alexandra Levit

12. *#MOJOtweet*: 140 Bite-Sized Ideas on How to Get and Keep Your Mojo by Marshall Goldsmith

13. *#PARTNER tweet Book01*: 140 Bite-Sized Ideas for Succeeding in Your Partnerships by Chaitra Vedullapalli

14. *#PROJECT MANAGEMENT tweet Book01*: 140 Powerful Bite-Sized Insights on Managing Projects by Guy Ralfe and Himanshu Jhamb

15. *#OPEN TEXTBOOK tweet Book01*: Driving the Awareness and Adoption of Open Textbooks by Sharyn Fitzpatrick

16. *#QUALITYtweet Book01*: 140 Bite-Sized Ideas to Deliver Quality in Every Project by Tanmay Vora

17. *#SOCIALMEDIA NONPROFIT tweet Book01*: 140 Bite-Sized Ideas fo Nonprofit Social Media Engagement by Janet Fouts with Beth Kanter

18. *#STANDARDStweet Book01*: 140 Bite-Sized Ideas for Winning the Industry Standards Game by Karen Bartleson

19. *#TEAMWORK tweet Book01*: 140 Powerful Bite-Sized Insights on Lessons for Leading Teams to Success by Caroline G. Nicholl

20. *#THINK tweet Book01*: Bite-sized lessons for a fast paced world by Rajesh Setty

www.ingramcontent.com/pod-product-compliance
Lightning Source LLC
Chambersburg PA
CBHW071215050326

40689CB00011B/2332